Zig-zag, buzz and hum!
Can a bug rap for fun?

2

Zig-zag, buzz and hum!
The bugs can rap for fun.

Zig-zag, buzz and hum!
Can a bug jam in the sun?

3

4

Zig-zag, rat-a-tat-tun!
A bug can jam in the sun.

Zig-zag, buzz and hug!
Can a cat cut a rug?

5

6

Zig-zag, rig-a-jig-jug!
A cat can cut a rug.

The bugs rap and jam!
A cat cuts a rug.

7

8

Zig-zag, rap and jam!
Cut a rug, FUN!

Just For Fun

Ask someone to help you read and do these activities.

Missing Words

Copy each sentence below. The last word in each sentence is missing.
Choose the correct word at the right to finish each sentence.
Write the word in the blank.

1. A bug can rap for _____.

   rug
   fun
   hum

2. A bug can jam in the _____.

   sun
   cut
   hug

3. A cat can cut a _____.

   fun
   rug
   sun

My Favorite Thing

1. Draw a picture of your favorite thing in the story.

2. Have someone help you write a sentence about your picture.

STECK
PHONICS READERS
VAUGHN

Zig-Zag, Buzz and Hum

STECK-VAUGHN
COMPANY
A Subsidiary of National Education Corporation

ISBN 0-8114-5153-4

90000

9 780811 451536

Tonka™

If I Could Drive an AMBULANCE!

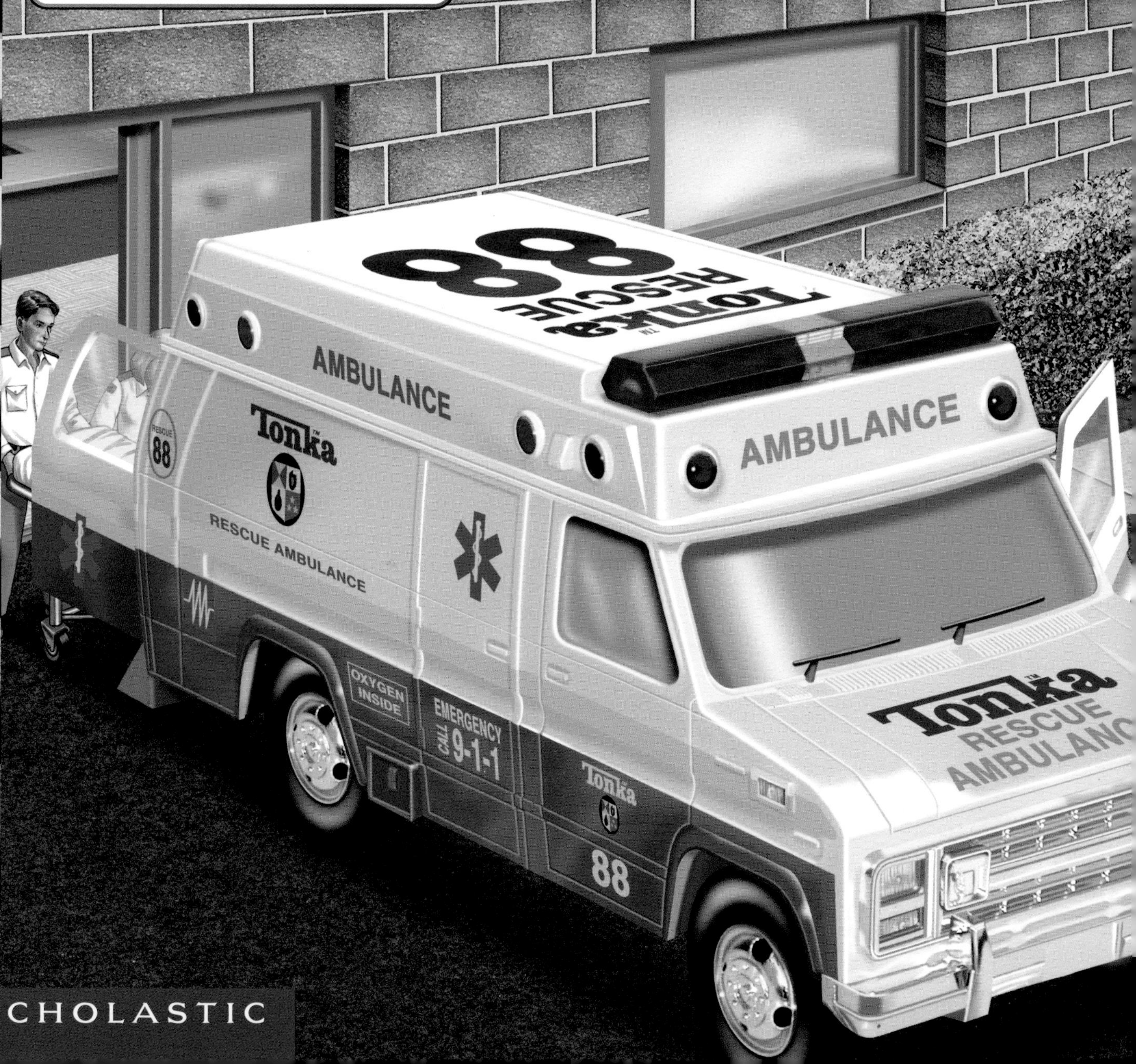

SCHOLASTIC

EAN

ISBN 0-439-44439-5

9 780439 444395

50350